# Birches

Also by Carl Adamshick

*Receipt*

*Saint Friend*

*Curses and Wishes*

# Birches

Carl Adamshick

Four Way Books
Tribeca

Library of Congress Cataloging-in-Publication Data

Names: Adamshick, Carl, 1969- author.
Title: Birches / Carl Adamshick.
Description: New York, NY : Four Way Books, 2019.
Identifiers: LCCN 2018028707 | ISBN 9781945588242 (pbk. : alk. paper)
Classification: LCC PS3601.D399 A6 2019 | DDC 811/.6--dc23
LC record available at https://lccn.loc.gov/2018028707

This book is manufactured in the United States of America and printed on acid-free paper.

Four Way Books is a not-for-profit literary press. We are grateful for the assistance we receive from individual donors, public arts agencies, and private foundations.

NEW YORK STATE OF OPPORTUNITY. | Council on the Arts

This publication is made possible with public funds from the New York State Council on the Arts, a state agency.

PROUD MEMBER
[clmp]

We are a proud member of the Community of Literary Magazines and Presses.

for Brother Dave, Nat, and Julie

Contents

# Black Snow

My brother sent a letter

from the house
where our mother is dying

He describes the planet earth
its trees and low buildings
wheeling past the sun

I picture him
in the plastic lawn chair
at the head of the driveway

a thistle growing
in the crack beside his beer bottle

leaving a wet ring
on the blonde cement

The tenuous frail night
landing like a paper airplane
in a field of high corn

Then fireflies
Then mosquitoes
pulling iron from his veins

# Language

If we had visitors from the future
come to hear what we had to say

I'm assuming the last thing I said
would be the first thing they heard

the first sound to enter
into their bodies of soft glass

and if they kept burrowing
through time

they would hear my first word last
then watch

as I squeeze myself into a ball
and give birth to my mother

# Black Snow

From my mother's funeral
I brought back Illinois

I brought back a ring and a necklace
I brought black snow

I brought a sense of cruelty
and rage that felt fair
to inflict on each moment

I brought back a new calendar
where the days
were ten times longer

and had to be opened
using tweezers on a dial
with a six-digit combination

# Moon Seen Through Windshield

If you are anything like I am
and I have faith that you are
then you have already stepped
out of your body
and been irrevocably wounded

I was born in 1969
Chances are you were born
during a different year
It doesn't matter if you were born
three thousand years ago

or if you are born
three thousand years from now
we share what it means to live

Maybe you have gone
back into your body

and found words
the only guide
into the known dark

We are both the living and the dead
the stuff beyond theory

Sometimes it is too much
and other times not enough

We wake to a morning fog
We wake to morning sun
We sit in a cold evening
thinking of the death of a parent

A different evening
has us thinking of our eyes
and how they crawled
out of our minds

at some point
in the evolution of the self

It is the evening of the first day
of a new year
I ask myself What have you done
The list is remarkable

# At the Crown Hotel

Most came down to the cafe
with friends—three or five
to a table

The waiter brought coffee
and took dishes
with such purpose

for someone having
a few days earlier
survived a suicide

# Black Snow

I live between the bus stop
and something I can't explain,
between the night sounding
with green leaves and a few
visible stars, between a horse
and philosophy wondering
if it is a great clenched fist
that keeps me from my life.
Now I live between my mother's
death and my own. I close
my eyes and see a different
darkness. Under the trees
wind falls through my hair.
You were a place, Mother.
I've always wanted to be a place,
a destination with a park bench.
I'm afraid I'm only the weather.
Night is miles off approaching
like a storm. I've sat so long
it is like traveling. I've watched
the sun move out of the shade
and the shade move into the sun.

# Moonlit Glass

I miss everyone. I miss my friend
Matthew and his appetite for acceptance,
his kindness, exuberance, his way
of making me happy in a world
that snows. I miss my mother,
whose first birthday after her death
is today. I miss the red maple
in her front yard giving
its leaves to October. I miss
my brother who says the kitchen,
not the bedroom, is the great room
of intimacy. I miss the sky
because I once read Hikmet
list the cosmos as something
he didn't know he loved.
I've spent the day discovering
that things I want and things I don't
wear the same clothes.
I miss my ex, would still spend
an afternoon with her talking,
would still sleep with her
if she wanted to lose
her grasp of language in a mess
of cotton sheets. I spent my youth

in church not believing
but feeling unified after service,
liking the white cars in the lot
and the dogs behind the chain link.
Tonight, on the shelf, a glass moose
figurine holds in its left antler
a tiny reflection of the moon
that is somehow shooting through
and illuminating its whole body.
It reminds me of how I used
to think of blood as its own being,
as a creature searching for a way out.
I take the moose from the shelf.
It goes dark in my hand.
It has no eyes, has no ears or mind.
It has no mouth, but then
its mother never had children.

# Estrangement

I live in your umbrella
standing on a sea of dirt.
The white light of noon
blasting like a bullhorn.

I've done so much without you
I want to share.

# Weakness

I want what you want
I've always wanted what you've wanted

# New Moon

Some movie had come out
while my mother was in hospice.
Nurses talked about the lead,
how sexy he was, a saxophonist
in the fifties, wore a sharp suit
with a razor-thin tie, gentle
with eyes that kept going.
They showed me how to fold
sheets in such a way
that when I changed them
my mother didn't have to leave
the bed. I wanted to be a nurse.
I wanted to go into houses
and help people die, which
is what I was doing, except
my mother wasn't a stranger,
she was my mother. And my
family was there, which was
making it easier and much more
difficult. I would heavily salt
fried onions because that is what
she loved. I would take the car
and get her chocolate caramel
explosion malts I didn't want

to give her because that is
what she loved. Her hands
were beautiful. A neighbor's
daughter came and did her nails
a Halloween orange, dyed
her hair, waxed her lip.
My mother told me the summer
she looked best in a two-piece
was 1963. Then apologized
for saying it. She was married twice,
each for a span of twenty years.
Each man was my father,
but one of them wasn't.
To tell you the truth,
the movie came out four
months after my mother's
death and they weren't nurses
but friends talking about the lead.
I went to see the movie. It was
beautiful and sad, the choices
and commitments were real
and devastating. The man *was* sexy,
more a minor character. I did
wish to be alive in black and white

playing a horn like him, my history
stretching back only an hour
to the opening credits where
everything before them collapsed
into nothingness, into no-story,
into something to sleep through,
something to avoid by sleeping.
I'm thankful she let me be close
to her dying. It was a gift,
not a gift really, it was how
she took care of me, always
showing me how it is going to be.
My brother, my one brother
who couldn't handle the moon
sliding over our mother's face
took to driving and parking
on the shoulders of highways.
When I watched the movie
and saw the woman walking
back to the convent to maybe
take her vows and become a nun
because outside the cloistered
walls was insane, I thought
of my brother. I wished

he was with me, that we were
watching the movie together
even if the theater was empty
and the projector didn't have
a bulb.

# Midnight

I started the year
in sleep, a dark accomplishment.
The world held at bay.

Like always, everything
will happen this year.
Accidents. Marriages.

Moments will wash us
or muddy our being.
It will be difficult. Easy.

I woke and saw
how the future has always
wanted to be intimate.

I pan-fry a slice of bread,
spoon sour cream
onto the warm crumb.

Sometimes it takes
everything one has
to say something.

# Flashlight

I think of how many lives we live
in this one life and how in every
one of them silence is misunderstood.
I think of my mother and how
I'm under the holy bell of her movie,
under her narrative, that film
she played over and over in the dark
of her brain while she waited,
while her real life slid by uninterrupted.
I have the same trouble explaining
this place, of always getting in my own
way. I see the kitchen table with relatives
and friends talking through and over
one another, I hear a song
from the record collection that hasn't
seen a new album in ten years,
but can't see the table for what it is,
a surface stacked with newspapers
and mail with no place to sit or eat.
I wake at 4:30, stumble into the cold
world of snow and stars to clear ice
from the truck thinking of nights
when I was younger, how they
would break open like names,

and how when you looked inside
you felt air rushing out. Somehow,
I've left the flashlight on the bench
in the truck's cab, its saucer of dim
light sleeping on the rough fabric.
I see the town where I grew up
in a shadowbox. The trees are made
of paper, the inhabitants tiny lights.
It's evening in the box of the world.
The houses have windows and doors
of ink, the church a burnished gold nib,
a bishop's hat on top of a foil candy-
wrapper spire. I see what you see
only different. I see what my mother
saw only different. I remember summer
storm clouds seen out a second-story
bedroom window—crawling over a field
of spring corn. I dislike and am confused
by what I tell myself, like how peaceful
this morning's quiet black resting
on the field's wide white wing is
or how my first love lacked only a bed,
a car and a job. I tell myself
whatever is falling through my body

falls out of optimism. I see my mother
in the last shirt she would ever wear,
a shirt picked out from a hundred shirts
in her closet, a shirt cut in the back
from hem to collar. I do what
I'm supposed to do. I do what I *think*
I'm supposed to do. I remember her
standing on a picnic table, the brim
of a baseball cap shading her right ear,
yelling for her oldest son to win.
Soon she will walk through the front
door in her chest. Often, I think
of only myself and what I've done.
I feel like a blockade, a checkpoint
where I ask for papers at a mysterious
gate and then deny myself access
into the country of my own existence.

# Moon Seen Two Days Before Thanksgiving

My mother is the glass cabinet
with snow falling

to the floor of her body

What I mean to say is
she has just died

everything

I can't say hello
I say hello

# Black Snow

I came home
from my mother's funeral

to a house of my own making

to dust I didn't want
to lift from a shelf

I came home astonished
by life being the same

struck dumb
when the knife
sunk into the melon

# Armistice

Before I changed my mother
for the first time
she asked me to call the pharmacy
thinking the woman
always dressed in the store's dark
blue could come spare us.
I said: *Ma we knew this was coming.*
*Then call Kim,* she says,
but her friend Kim is wearing
an apron and walking circles
in a restaurant with a coffee pot
and won't be able to help
with the necessaries.
Kim is all of us—
living with our own concerns,
conquered by adulthood,
love playing the part
of a winter coat lost
in the immensity. Kim
and the woman who puts
the pills in the bottle,
and all my old high-school
friends working, unable to stay
late around the bonfire. The nurses

had schedules and uniforms.
My mother's bed was in the center
of the living room. Her morphine,
a viscous blue liquid I dropped
on her tongue. In the evenings,
Billie Holiday eased herself
out of the speakers and then sat
her voice down quietly
in the lamplight. I wanted
the nurses, regardless
of gender or age, to hold me
in the dark, to lie with me
on a bed of forgetfulness.
Many of them said:
*It's okay. She did it for you,*
*now you can return the favor.*
*It's the same.* But one nurse said:
*It is not the same.*

# Black Snow

I don't want to sit
at the table

don't want to talk or hear

how much the refrigerator
might be worth

# Taylor

I call Taylor when I need
to get out of the house,
when watching my mother
die while she watches
a Bears game becomes
too sad or boring or feels
like someone else
already paid for dinner.
My mother thinks Taylor
is wild, too free with strangers
and the drugs she uses,
that she can't make the right
choice, will always choose
the wrong man, that she has
no future but dark hours
of unhappiness and desolation,
crying in parking lots,
in ruin with no place to turn,
used up, having to walk home
with one busted heel. I ask
Taylor if she needs anything
before I come over. Once
she asked if I could bring

lettuce for Floppy, a grayish
bunny that sits in her lap
during movies. Tonight,
we watch *Men in Black*.
Taylor sits on the couch
with a pink translucent bong.
The movie starts. We talk
every so often. She can't wait
to move into the condos
being built along the Fox River.
Their rooms glisten and rotate
like cars in a showroom.
The movie has a gross bug
person and then a stadium
turns into a spaceship.
I've had most of a six-pack,
listened to water in the bong
graduate. The movie ends,
Taylor stands and stretches,
looks out the window
down onto the wet street
and asks if I want to watch
the movie again. There is

a button on this device
the men in black carry
that can make people forget
their entire lives.

# Moonlight Seen in Kitchen Sink

I like to think my mother
didn't die, that for her
everyone else passed
into oblivion

and she found herself
walking out the front door
only to open and sit

in her car, light a cigarette
in the evening that came
earlier in the afternoon.

Her shift starts
in twenty-five minutes,
she cracks the window,

turns the key in the ignition,
puts the car in reverse
and takes her foot
off the brake.

Her children are elsewhere.
She is out of her marriage,
has not yet entered another.
The house is cold.

Before swinging
the sedan into the street,
she stops, thinks, places
the car in park.

Back inside
she sees moonlight
in the kitchen sink,
flips on the lights,
picks up the phone
and calls in sick.

# Aubade

As we walked this morning
I believed everything you said

Sometimes the world is so simple
you can see all the way to the end

When we were on your steps
I noticed my green sweater
rolled up at your wrists

# Ornament

I'm there
the night my father is born
Lake Michigan
The basement
with a model train set
a rail yard full of cars
bearing German names

There he is at church
light in the apse
in the city that will teach him
everything
he won't be able to forget
He lights candles
His bicycle
black on the grass
black on the towpath
one pedal dug into the earth
black in the fallen leaves

That evening he kisses someone
a blanket of water
tucked in the street
He is unable to say
on his walk home
if the burning zodiac
is above the cloud cover
or under it like fish

His body wants the world
He imagines he can withstand
the concussions
of heat radiating
from all its living things
His body
a well-muscled perfection
wants to know sex
His thumb touches
the head of his penis
like it's a soft white mouse

He has children
I am not one of them
until much later
He is affectionate
gentle and caring
until my body
grows to the size
of his body

He steps away from tradition
Then there is no tree
to hang an ornament
only reasons for other reasons

Night is showing its teeth

He hears a woman
memorizing lines
behind the curtain of marriage
After the divorce
he lives like an anchor
albeit unaware he is the iron star
lowered into the water
to keep the ship in its berth

He smokes cigarettes
at the kitchen table
Drinks coffee
Has gray stubble
His knuckled heart
unclenching

He comes home to his body
a good man
He has never done
anything wrong
He has also never
done anything right
He is sunlight filling
a room as an idea
furthering itself
He has years
He has months
He has what days
he has

# On the Walk Home the Moon, Maybe, Probably, Somewhere

Heavily clouded evening sky.
No rain. Thought mostly
of that twenty-six-year-old's ass
with its tiny, tufted mercy
and how her mouth crumpled
when she asked about my mother.

# Black Snow

I want to tell you
how lonely it is
without her

mostly because
no one asks

My tongue a bank
of fog in the birches

I don't know
what it's like to live here

If this is the world
why don't I know

where my body ends

# Safari Moon

My mother had a schnoodle,
a dog like marshmallows
rolled in shaved coconut.
My brother and I drove,
mid-December, a minivan
loaded with furniture
westward through too
many states. The dog
slept on top of a desk
wound in an afghan
that smelled of our
mother's house. Her ashes
were in the back too,
in a box not large enough
to hold her lungs.
Monday in Iowa I thought
of her fingernails brushed
with Strawberry Pearl
or Safari Moon,
her silvery tray lined
with tiny bottles of polish.
We stopped for gas,
bought lottery tickets, which
was something we thought

she would have done.
We just kept losing.
*I don't care where I rest.*
*Put me in a river coming off*
*a mountain,* she had said.
She had never been
to the mountains.
I couldn't understand.
When it comes to dice
there's only one way
to roll snake eyes.
Outside Salt Lake City
I mourned my mother's
teeth and hair—moonlight,
snow and night filling
the bowl of the city.
When my brother and I
were home we unloaded
the van. I said goodbye
to the dog, goodbye
to my brother, put her
ashes on a shelf and fell
asleep wearing my clothes
on a blue couch.

It’s been almost a year
and she is still up there.
Sometimes, I picture her
as light, a zoo of light,
as wild shifting halations
trapped in a paper urn
and feel bad she is not
in the river. Then
it seems representative,
that what she did
was wait, that one’s
whole life could be spent
waiting, like all our last
words should be *I made it.*

# Branch Water

God has never said anything to me
and whenever someone says God
said something to them
I don't believe it.
What I mean is
I've never been to New Orleans
but I've read Stan Rice.
Sometimes after I've had a few
I wish I was with him
drinking warmed whiskey
from eggshells or from the mouth
of a silk-skinned messenger.
I can't believe they can believe.
Yet I saw my mother
put on a wristwatch,
saw it tick forward
for a minute and then
begin clicking backward.
We were in Kansas,
dusk and kicked-up dirt
fuzzed the sky. Stan
is a drunken scroll
unfurling down Broadway.
He is a balm. A narcotic.

Sobriety's anodyne.
If we were together
I would tell him
about the time I saw
his inner child as a ghost.
His cellophane skull lost
in Anne's black hair.
But he is dead. I can't
tell him anything.
In that way I am like God
and he is like one of his
paintings, an image
extracted from the dirt-
eating village of his brain.
I'd say Stan you were lucky.
Although I'm sorry
you had to clean the dog
teeming with lavender spiders.
I know I'm reducing
my life to a few sentences
and that it is a great mystery
I am not what I have written.
I think Stan would tell me
drama is Greek for fake

and that we are dumb
archaeologists stumbling
through a dig site
with preconceived notions
that each word is a bone
or fragment of bone
and it's inevitable
we conclude, judging
from the structure
and philology, that the animal
resembled a closed book.
I don't know if Stan
wanted to continue
or what his cosmology
was. Maybe he thought
silence was a window
open to the mountain air,
a transparent map
showing the ocean floor
and the lost city
where his child grew tall.
Maybe he thought memory
was the water he could hear
on the mountain

as he pushed the silence
closed. Leukemia
getting its fill
at the all-you-can-eat
buffet of his daughter.

# Cortège

Let that be everything
let it be over
Forgiveness is arrogant
and contentious
Cars glint under cemetery trees
There are so many ways
to become ugly

# Black Snow

My mother died
on the twenty-sixth

two days before Thanksgiving
In two years

the twenty-sixth
will be on Thanksgiving

I don't understand the moon

Does it really circle back
Isn't time a field

like grief
expanding to the horizon

Trees mute in their MRIs

Couldn't it be October
instead of now

# Black Snow

Like language and death

the tongue is not connected
at one of its ends

# The Distance Between Things Can't Be Seen

My mother tells me
I have to tell her
when she has to stop
dyeing her hair.

Everything can become so unmanageable.

Clouds bunched above the city.

She is picking me up at the airport.
Last time I was home
I regressed to a thing
watching television

and instead of seeing friends
kept choosing to stay in
and make out with a bag of chips.

She wants to meet me curbside
after I grab my luggage.

When I get there she is in baggage claim.
We walk back to the car.
We sit in the car for a minute

while she holds the wheel,
then mumbles *I'm safe now.*

There is so much in the world
I want to understand.

Once in school we watched
tadpoles grow feet
and lose their tails.
We were allowed to have one.

I remember weeping
when my frog died.
I promised to be the mother
in every situation.

# Weather

What an embarrassment
most of life is—

people seeing everything.

Do we really spend our days
hiding, unable to face
ourselves, not wanting

to hurt others
and hurting them.

Sunlight on the table,
memory a room I've decorated
many times—still unsatisfied.

I've always known
I would live a portion
of life without my parents,

but never knew how that would feel.

God, aka, the unknown,
i.e. death, help us.

The stars are sitting down for dinner.

I've lost my mother
and keep losing her
as the weather changes.

An animal sleeping in its den
can resemble a brain.
I've lashed my mother
to what I am,
but she can't stay tied to me

like she couldn't tie her youngest
to herself and still be decent.

It can be a lifetime of armchairs
in rain-soaked fields.

Now I understand a friend
whose heart is cloud.

In sleep, I wrangle
open a damaged body,
unpack its heart,

place the contents on a table.
Each life lies there breathing.
The dead shine in crescents.

I feel the world is inside
an iron casement
floating under a bridge

on its way to a great swaying
city of salt, but I'm just sitting

on a small red throne
in a theater with the THX
hiking through my ears.

Outside other things are happening—
the magnolia for instance.

All day I went around
with the window
of my body open

and wasn't hurt.

## Moonlight in the Dark and Roving Troughs

Maybe you didn't know your mother.
Maybe she is still alive.
Maybe we don't know anyone.

I'm alive.
I find that undeniable
and my mother is what we have come
to define as dead.

She remains in that noun
like the moon remains itself.

Feelings pass through,
leave us, return, leave us
again empty
and then, again, we are waylaid

by their impossibility,
in the mercy
of the dark and roving troughs.

I didn't say enough about the chair.

I hated that chair.
It was my mother's university.
She sat there ten hours a day
for ten years,

all the chicken and hamburger
and sugar she devoured
while her dog ruined
the white leather,

all the shows and commercials,
all the prescription drugs
making the chair a spacecraft
she negotiated
through the rock of Saturn's rings.

Maybe when you are close
you can't love everything.
Maybe family is a tourniquet

and compassion only arrives
after and late

like a friend knocking
in the small hours.

If I could—if there was—
if my mother—if the tree
or night—

# Black Snow

Here is what is real
I held my mother's hand

sometimes

We talked

There was so much
that didn't happen

I don't want words
to make a fiction

Her death was much like her life

a battleground

Between what she saw
and what she thought

was her life
her body
the place
she lived

# Black Snow

The moon visits
when the moon
sits in darkness

# Salt

Everything we eat is dead

and we love
eating together.

My first ten thousand meals
were with my mother.

The first time alone
must have been awful—
a mineral sting
I can't remember.

I want experience
without the experience.
I want my mother alive,

but to have had the experience
of her dying.

I want to be green and black,
the two infinite colors.

It is almost spring.

Yesterday, I shared french fries
and a salad with a friend.

Today the mountain
is white marbled rose.
As the hours pass,

I watch it change
to the blue of wet, discarded
swim trunks and then, for a moment,
think it is invisible.

## Black Snow

My quiet mother
is dying. The summer tree
silent without wind.

# Concrete Mixer

I remember.
Meaning I am alive.
Meaning I have no idea
how a forest maintains
itself or how clouds
or the moon aren't different.
I remember deleting
my mother's phone number
from my phone
while sitting next to her.
She was sleeping.
A strange secret.
I prepared for her death
by preparing. Each day
had incremental losses.
Grief never overwhelmed
but suffused. The background
was sadness yet every hour,
even every second,
held the whole range
of emotions. A malt
did my mother in.
Her friend Pickles brought
what was called a concrete mixer,

my mother's favorite
concoction of ice cream
and crumbled candy bars.
The three of us talked.
My mother sitting up.
The waxed paper cup
resting on her chest,
its red spoon nestled
in the frozen cream.
The nurses, all of them,
kept saying patients let go
when they have everything,
when they are comfortable
and happy and at ease.
My mother was almost
half-done when the malt
slipped off her chest
and began to empty
between her arm and body
I said *Fuck Ma*
*what are you doing?*

*Ah Baby it spilled.*

I had just bathed her.
I grabbed a towel,
put the rest of the concrete
mixer in the freezer
and cleaned the gooey
melty mess. My mother
didn't talk after that.
I called everyone,
told them they better come
now before it's too late.
Pickles is Pickles
because Claussen is her last name.

# Light from a Blue Moon

When the credits rolled
on my mother's life
I was surprised by being
listed as a supporting actor

Really it's understandable

Most of her life was lived
without me and much
of mine I didn't share

Isn't that what she taught
to speak only when spoken to
Isn't that how I am
nothing to say unless asked

# Exactly Okay

My father is a ship
of moonlight
docked in the harbor
of a harvested
field. Beyond is a hill,

a wave of dirt, breaking
on a reef of the world.
My family is buried
out there. Although
it's not a cemetery
but a place made perfect

by not existing.
My mother wanted
to live an hour longer
than her second husband,
but he is still breathing
somewhere in Virginia.

I, too, want to live
by giving myself away.
Eventually, I will
give myself to death,

who will probably
make me stand in line

on a street of Mondays
before my real death
and its long hours begin.
I dreamed a commercial,

a time-lapsed video
of corn from sprout
to bearded tassel swaying
before the combine
with the bright overlaid
text: *Coca-Cola*.

In the procession
of leaves I see the tree's
principles, the tight
concentric logic,
the hidden cold maple
in the rings, how sometimes
things touch only themselves.

Autumn, everyone
with a light in their mouth.
The small things
making us happy,
how it's only special
when it's not meant
to be special—
knowing your envelope
keeping my place
in the *Collected Stories*
*of Elizabeth Spencer*
is one of them

and there's always Poland
in my mind, the painted
egg of Krakow. When
I think of yellow, I think
of mustards in glass jars
and white bowls and want a gold
Trans Am with a cream
and daffodil interior

I can park in the sunshine
of a Floridian Costco,
a do-it-yourself or Dior
colostomy bag to show
off like an only child.
It seems like a good way
to leave this world.

I feel exactly okay.
The great claims
having been undone.
In the woods, bright
as a flashlight,
I see the season close
down like a carnival,

hear my friends singing
from a rowboat parked
in their backyard,
their manhattans lit,
magically, from within,
feel my knuckles ring
out across the field
of my body and see

the bell of the nurse’s
stethoscope
who happened to work
the day I was born—
the little microphone
picking up the faint
sounds inside.

Everything opens
and falls to the bottom.
My mother is night
above an ocean.
Often I see her walking
toward me, a million
domains of light. The city
bus being driven
through the rain
is carrying neighbors
most of the way home.

The trees, along the way,
being just what they
are, their bare branches
signaling to one another.

The bus working
on the Sabbath. I love
how you rent a seat
like an apartment
or pay mortgage
on a three-bedroom
split-level mid-fifties
ranch. My friend
Jay in the back reading
above the wheel well.

Acknowledgments

*American Poetry Review, Columbia, Electric Lit, Los Angeles Review of Books, Provincetown Arts.*

Carl Adamshick lives in Portland, Oregon, where he works as editor of Tavern Books, a nonprofit publisher dedicated to poetry and the preservation of books and book culture. His published works include *Curses and Wishes*, recipient of the Walt Whitman Award from the Academy of American Poets, *Saint Friend,* and *Receipt*.

Publication of this book was made possible by grants and donations. We are also grateful to those individuals who participated in our 2018 Build a Book Program. They are:

Anonymous (11), Sally Ball, Vincent Bell, Jan Bender-Zanoni, Kristina Bicher, Laurel Blossom, Adam Bohanon, Betsy Bonner, Mary Brancaccio, Lee Briccetti, Jane Martha Brox, Carla & Steven Carlson, Caroline Carlson, Stephanie Chang, Tina Chang, Liza Charlesworth, Andrea Cohen, Machi Davis, Marjorie Deninger, Patrick Donnelly, Charles Douthat, Emily Flitter, Lukas Fauset, Monica Ferrell, Jennifer Franklin, Helen Fremont & Donna Thagard, Robert Fuentes & Martha Webster, Ryan George, Panio Gianopoulos, Chuck Gillett, Lauri Grossman, Julia Guez, Naomi Guttman & Jonathan Mead, Steven Haas, Lori Hauser, Mary & John Heilner, Ricardo Hernandez, Deming Holleran, Nathaniel Hutner, Janet Jackson, Rebecca Kaiser Gibson, David Lee, Jen Levitt, Howard Levy, Owen Lewis, Sara London & Dean Albarelli, David Long, Katie Longofono, Cynthia Lowen, Ralph & Mary Ann Lowen, Jacquelyn Malone, Fred Marchant, Donna Masini, Catherine McArthur, Nathan McClain, Richard McCormick, Victoria McCoy, Britt Melewski, Kamilah Moon, Beth Morris, Rebecca Okrent, Gregory Pardlo, Veronica Patterson, Jill Pearlman, Marcia & Chris Pelletiere, Maya Pindyck, Megan Pinto, Taylor Pitts, Eileen Pollack, Barbara Preminger, Kevin Prufer, Vinode Ramgopal, Martha Rhodes, Peter & Jill Schireson, Jason Schneiderman, Jane Scovel, Andrew Seligsohn & Martina Anderson, Soraya Shalforoosh, James Snyder & Krista Fragos, Ann St. Claire, Alice St. Claire-Long, Dorothy Tapper Goldman, Robin Taylor, Marjorie & Lew Tesser, Boris Thomas, Judith Thurman, Susan Walton, Calvin Wei, Bill Wenthe, Allison Benis White, Elizabeth Whittlesey, Rachel Wolff, Hao Wu, Anton Yakovlev, and Leah Zander.